This book

_____

_____

_____

_____

Written and compiled by
Sophie Piper
Illustrations copyright © 2010
Mique Moriuchi
This edition copyright © 2010
Lion Hudson

The moral rights of the author and
illustrator have been asserted

A Lion Children's Book
an imprint of
Lion Hudson plc
Wilkinson House, Jordan Hill Road,
Oxford OX2 8DR, England
www.lionhudson.com
ISBN 978 0 7459 6929 9

First edition 2010
10 9 8 7 6 5 4 3 2 1 0

Acknowledgments
Every effort has been made to
trace and contact copyright owners
for material used in this book.
We apologize for any inadvertent
omissions or errors.

All unattributed prayers are by
Sophie Piper and Lois Rock,
copyright © Lion Hudson.
The prayer on page 20 by
Christina Goodings is copyright
© Lion Hudson.

Bible extracts are taken or adapted
from the Good News Bible,
published by The Bible Societies/
HarperCollins Publishers Ltd,
UK © American Bible Society
1966, 1971, 1976, 1992, used by
permission.

A catalogue record for this book is
available from the British Library

Typeset in 18/20 Lapidary 333 BT
Printed in China April 2010
(manufacturer LH06)

Distributed by:
UK: Marston Book Services Ltd,
PO Box 269, Abingdon, Oxon
OX14 4YN
USA: Trafalgar Square Publishing,
814 N Franklin Street, Chicago,
IL 60610
USA Christian Market: Kregel
Publications, PO Box 2607,
Grand Rapids, MI 49501

Prayers for a Better World

Sophie Piper
Mique Moriuchi

LION
CHILDREN'S

Looking at the sky
while a tall tree sways,
I hear God speaking
in a thousand different ways:
of melodies and miracles
that all are born on earth;
of dreams and possibilities
of everlasting worth.

Contents

6

For Planet Earth

Here on the ancient rock of earth
I sit and watch the sky;
I feel the breeze that moves the trees
While stately clouds float by.
I wonder why our planet home
Spins round and round the sun
And what will last for ever
When earth's days all are done.

Earth

The earth is born of long ago
when to a shapeless night
of storm and never-ending dark
God said, "Let there be light."

We think the earth is ours.

We dig it, drill it, plough it, mine it,
pave it.

Then, from within the heart of things,
the earth erupts. It shakes, it quakes,
it shifts, it drifts.

May we learn to respect the earth, for it
is shaped by forces greater than our own,
and we should live in awe of them.

Ocean

Pearly seashell,
filled with brine,
can your ocean
all be mine?

Pilgrim, no:
for sea and shore
belong to God
for evermore.

River

Let us learn how the rivers dance:

let us watch how they trickle and surge,
how they fall and curl,
how they swirl and eddy.

Let us see how they dance according
to the rules God gave them; how they
are more obedient to their Maker than
any of humankind.

Let us learn from the rivers how to
dance to the Maker's tune.

Sun

The sunrise
tells of God's glory;
the moonrise
tells of God's glory;
the starshine
tells of God's glory;
the heavens
tell of God's glory.

Based on Psalm 19

O God,
You are more splendid than the lights that
   shine across the universe.
You are more powerful than forces that
   scatter the stars.
You whisper to me more gently than the
   night-time breeze.
Your blessings are as sure as the sunrise.

Year

In winter, God takes a sheet of plain
paper and pencils in the outline of things.

In spring, God brings out a paintbox and
washes the background in blue and green
and yellow.

In summer, God adds bright details: pink
and red and orange and mauve.

In the autumn, God scatters golden glitter.

May planet earth
go round and round
yet may our dreams
be heaven bound.

17

For Creatures Great and Small

He prayeth best, who loveth best
All things both great and small;
For the dear God who loveth us,
He made and loveth all.

S. T. Coleridge (1772–1834)

Little things

Create a space for little things:
Bejewelled bugs with buzzing wings

And pudgy grubs that bravely cling
To slender stems that bend and swing.

Create a calm for quiet things:
For timid birds too shy to sing

And breaths of wind that softly linger
In the blossom trees of spring.

Christina Goodings

Glimpses of heaven

I think the butterfly
says her prayer
by simply fluttering
in the air.

I think the prayer
of the butterfly
just dances up
to God on high.

If you have heard
the sound of birdsong
in the morning air,
then you will know
that heaven's music
reaches everywhere.

Birds

God bless the birds of springtime
that twitter in the trees
and flutter in the hedgerows
and soar upon the breeze.

God bless the birds of summer
that gather on the shore
and glide above the ocean
where breakers crash and roar.

God bless the birds of autumn
as they prepare to fly
and fill the damp and chilly air
with wild and haunting cry.

God bless the birds of winter
that hop across the snow
and peck the fallen seeds and fruits
of summer long ago.

Diversity

Multicoloured animals
With stripes and dots and patches:
God made each one different –
There isn't one that matches.

I think of the diverse majesty
Of all of the creatures on earth
Some with the power to terrify
Others that only bring mirth
I think of their shapes and their colours
Their secret and curious ways
And my heart seems to yearn for a
   language
To sing their Great Maker's praise.

Wild

God of the mountain,
God of the plain:
may the wild creatures run freely again.

God of the forest,
God of the glade:
shelter the creatures in leafy green shade.

God of the harvest,
God of the seed:
may the world's creatures have all that
    they need.

For Green and Growing Things

I plant a tree for the earth.
I plant a tree for the air.
I plant a tree for the whole wide world
that God gave us all to share.

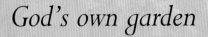

God's own garden

God is a fierce gardener:
clearing the overgrown world
with fire and flood,
with windstorm and landslide.

God is a gentle gardener:
clothing the bare earth
with trailing tendrils
and tiny flowers.

God is all powerful; God is all love.

Flowers

Dear God,
We give you thanks for the beautiful plants
you deliver to our garden from the fields
and the woodlands.

All is well:
the leaves of grass are growing.
All is well:
the leaves of flowers are showing.
All is well:
the leaves of trees are blowing.
All is well:
God's springtime love is showing.

Harvests

The harvest of our garden
is astonishingly small;
but oh, dear God, we thank you
that there's anything at all.

Lord, help those who plant and sow,
weed and water, rake and hoe,
toiling in the summer heat
for the food they need to eat.

Bless the work of their tired hands:
turn their dry and dusty lands
to a garden, green and gold,
as their harvest crops unfold.

Trees

The trees grow down,
down into the earth,
right down into long ago.

The trees grow up,
up into the sky,
right up where the strong winds blow.

The trees, they sway,
they sway in the wind
and whisper a secret song:

"We thank you, God,
for keeping us safe,
that we might grow tall and strong."

Mending, not ending

Our world is broken
and we must mend it.

It is our home;
we dare not end it.

The earth lies bare
so we shall tend it.

We pray for help:
and God will send it.

For Peace and Justice

We share the earth
we share the sky
we share the shining sea
with those we trust
with those we fear:
we are God's family.

43

Friends

Dear God,
guard our friendships:

Encourage us,
that we may encourage one another.

Inspire us,
that we may inspire one another.

Strengthen us,
that we may strengthen one another.

Remember us,
that we may remember one another.

Forgiving

From the mud
a pure white flower

From the storm
a clear blue sky

As we pardon
one another

God forgives us
from on high.

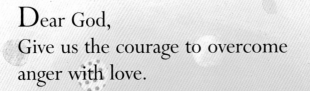

Dear God,
Give us the courage to overcome
anger with love.

Hands around the world

We
not me.

Share
not tear.

Mend
not end

and so
befriend.

O God,
Gather together as one
those who believe in peace.
Gather together as one
those who believe in justice.
Gather together as one
those who believe in love.

Swords into ploughshares

O God,
Settle the quarrels among the nations.

May they hammer their swords into ploughs
and their spears into pruning knives…

Where the tanks now roll, let there be
    tractors;
where the landmines explode, let the fields
    grow crops.

Let there be a harvest of fruit and grain
and peace that all the world can share.

Based on Micah 4:3–5

For a World Made New

Hold on
to what you believe in –
though it be a tree on the windswept
   plain.

Dream on
for what you believe in –
though it be a seed on the trampled
   ground.

Patterns

O God,
You set the patterns of the world –
summer and winter,
seedtime and harvest –
so that all living things may flourish.

But we have been greedy
for warmth in wintertime
cool air in summertime
harvest crops at seedtime
spring flowers as the year grows old.

Teach us to live peaceably with the world.
Let the patterns be restored
and bless us.

Somewhere to be

Save me a clean stream, flowing
to unpolluted seas;

lend me the bare earth, growing
untamed flowers and trees.

May I share safe skies
when I wake, every day,

with birds and butterflies?
Grant me a space where I can play

with water, rocks, trees, and sand;
lend me forests, rivers, hills, and sea.

Keep me a place in this old land,
somewhere to grow, somewhere to be.

Jane Whittle

Old and new

Thank you, dear God,
for the blessing of things that stay the same:
for the people we have known for ever
and the familiar paths where we walk.

Thank you, dear God,
for the blessing of things that change:
for newcomers with their new customs,
new ways of doing things, new paths
    to discover.

Thank you, dear God,
for the blessing of the old and the blessing
    of the new.

What to do with the world

Enjoy the world with your feet:
walk it.

Enjoy the world with your hands:
touch it.

Enjoy the world with your eyes:
admire it.

Enjoy the world with your nose:
smell it.

Enjoy the world with your ears:
listen to its music.

Enjoy the world with your whole body:
live in it.

61

Index of first lines